HEALING
it is
ALWAYS
God's Will

Study Guide

KENNETH COPELAND

HEALING

it is

ALWAYS

God's Will

>=∘> Study Guide <∘=<

KENNETH COPELAND

KENNETH COPELAND
PUBLICATIONS

Healing
It Is Always God's Will
Study Guide

ISBN-10 1-57562-712-4   30-0732
ISBN-13 978-1-57562-712-0

23 22 21 20 19 18   9 8 7 6 5

Kenneth Copeland Publications
Fort Worth, TX 76192-0001

For more information about Kenneth Copeland Ministries, visit kcm.org or call 1-800-600-7395 (U.S. only) or +1-817-852-6000.

1

"*Surely he hath borne our griefs, and carried our sorrows: yet we did esteem him stricken, smitten of God, and afflicted.*"

Isaiah 53:4

To receive healing a believer must make a quality decision that is based on faith in The Word of God.

CD ONE
Healing—Is It God's Will?

To Receive Healing From God, You Must Know That It Is the Will of God to Heal

The Healing Power of God

FOCUS: The healing power of God is a spiritual force. This force is constant. The Anointing of God to heal is a reality and is always available.

God's power to heal is governed by spiritual law. Through the knowledge of His Word and applications of it in faith, God's healing power will operate. In Hosea 4:6, God said that His people are destroyed for a lack of knowledge. It is important for us, as believers, to make ourselves knowledgeable concerning healing.

To receive healing from God, you must *know* that it is the will of God to heal. The Word of God is His will. John 5:30 says, "I [Jesus] can of mine own self do nothing: as I hear, I judge: and my judgement is just; because I seek not mine own will, but the will of the Father which hath sent me." Jesus was the visible representation of the invisible God (Colossians 1:15, *AMPC*). Everything that Jesus said and did was an expression of the Father's will (see John 6:38).

> *The Anointing of God to heal is a reality and is always available.*

The power to heal was present in Jesus' earthly ministry. In Acts 10:38, the Bible says that God anointed Jesus of Nazareth with the Holy Ghost and *power,* "...who [Jesus] went about doing good, and healing all that were oppressed of the devil; for God was with him."

First of all, we see that sickness and oppression are works of the devil. God is not the cause of sickness and disease. If He were, then Jesus would never have gone to the cross to pay the dear price He did for us to be well.

Secondly, Jesus was anointed to heal *all* who were oppressed of the devil. He was executing the will of God in the earth. He is the same, yesterday, today and forever (Hebrews 13:8). He was carrying out God's will then and is carrying it out today in the lives of believers who activate The Word in faith.

Receiving healing from God takes a decision of quality. It must be based on The Word of God. The believer must base his faith on The Word and not on the testimony of another believer who was healed. He cannot allow himself to be shaken in his confidence because of someone who did not receive. When a man receives The Word as God's revealed will for his personal life and puts his trust in God's integrity, he will tap in to the power of God. He will walk in health.

"For the law of the Spirit of life *in Christ Jesus* hath made me free from the law of sin and death" (Romans 8:2). This is the express will of God. When a man receives salvation, he becomes a new creation *in Christ* (2 Corinthians 5:17). The *law* of the Spirit of life *in Christ* has set him *free* from the bondage of sin and death.

The Body of Christ should be as adamantly opposed to sickness and disease as it is opposed to sin. When Jesus took our punishment for sin, He bore our sickness and carried our diseases, fulfilling the words in Isaiah 53:4 (also see Matthew 8:17). The price for healing was paid for by the same sacrifice that paid for sin. Redemption was a complete work.

Now Begin Enjoying It

God has already laid out the paths He has chosen for us to walk in. It is now up to each individual to make the choice to walk in His ways by faith in His Word.

CD 1 Outlined

I. Healing power of God
  A. A spiritual force
    1. Constant; reality
    2. Available
  B. Operated by spiritual law
    1. Law of Spirit of life in Christ has freed us from the law of sin and death (Romans 8:2)

II. Receiving from God must be based on knowledge of God's will
  A. God's Word is His will
  B. Jesus manifested the will of God (John 5:30)
  C. God's will is healing—always
    1. See: Acts 10:38; John 14:10; Matthew 4:23, 8:16, 9:35, 12:15, 14:14; Luke 4:40

III. Receiving from God requires a quality decision
  A. Making a choice (Deuteronomy 30:19)
  B. Standing against sickness and disease

IV. Jesus set the Church against sickness and disease
  A. Mark 16:17-18

Study Questions

(1) What governs the operation of the healing power of God? _____

_____

_____

_____

(2) How can a person know what the will of God is concerning his healing? _____

_____

_____

_____

*(3) Is it **always** the will of God to heal?* _____

_____

_____

_____

*(4) Give several scripture references showing that Jesus healed **all** who were sick. Can you find other evidence in The Word concerning God's will for healing?* _____·_____

_____

_____

_____

_____

(5) Explain how redemption is a complete work. _____

_____

_____

_____

Study Notes

"For the law of the Spirit of life in Christ Jesus hath
made me free from the law of sin and death."
Romans 8:2

2

"*Beloved, I wish above all things that thou mayest prosper and be in health, even as thy soul prospereth.*"

3 John 2

Being *saved* is more than
salvation from eternal damnation.
It's being made whole—spirit, soul and body.

CD TWO
Healing Redemption

You Can Receive Healing by the Power of God, the Same Way You Received Eternal Life at the New Birth

Prosperity of the Soul

FOCUS: Man is a spirit being. He does not *have* a spirit, he *is* a spirit. He has a soul, which is the mind, will and emotions, and he lives in a body.

The Apostle Paul wrote in 1 Thessalonians 5:23, "And the very God of peace sanctify you *wholly;* and I pray God your *whole* spirit and soul and body be preserved blameless unto the coming of our Lord Jesus Christ."

One of the reasons why Christians have not enjoyed the benefit of healing for their bodies is that they have received salvation as being only the new birth. The Greek word for *save* in the New Testament is *sozo.* It not only means salvation from eternal damnation, but it means to be delivered from both spiritual and temporal evils; protected; made whole or sound—spirit, soul and body.

A man will prosper and be in health as his soul prospers (see Joshua 1:8; 3 John 2). A prosperous soul is one in which the mind is renewed to The Word of God and the will of God. Mind renewal is the result of meditating on God's Word. To receive healing from God, it is vital for the believer to accept The Word of God as his evidence and not what he perceives from his five senses.

> *To receive healing from God, it is vital for the believer to accept The Word of God as his evidence and not what he perceives from his five senses.*

The Word says, "Surely he [Jesus] hath borne our griefs and carried our sorrows: yet we did esteem him stricken, smitten of God, and afflicted. But he was wounded [tormented] for our transgressions, he was bruised for our iniquities: the chastisement of our peace was upon him; and with his stripes [or bruises] we are healed (Isaiah 53:4-5). The literal translation of *griefs* and *sorrows* is "sicknesses, weaknesses, pains and diseases." Jesus bore our sicknesses and carried our diseases at the same time He bore our sins. The Cross of Calvary provided for healing just as surely as it saved us from the punishment of sin. The redemption of man is all-inclusive. The Cross left no area of man's life to Satan's dominion. It covered the entire scope of human need.

Jesus never sinned. But in His substitutionary sacrifice, He was *made to be* sin that we might *be made* the righteousness of God in Him (2 Corinthians 5:21). He suffered with every sickness and disease known to man to make us well.

Healing is listed as a benefit of the Lord in Psalm 103. It is an act of kindness from the Lord for your well-being. Verse 3 says, "Who forgiveth *all* thine iniquities; who healeth *all* thy diseases…." Jesus demonstrated the same power to heal a man sick with palsy by saying, "Man, thy sins are forgiven thee." He asked the scribes and Pharisees which would be easier, to tell him his sins were forgiven; or to rise, take up his bed and walk? (See Luke 5:18-24.)

When The Word says we are to be partakers of Christ's sufferings, it simply means we are to enter in to the victory that Jesus has given us through the cross. To enter in to that victory, we encounter spiritual sufferings. This suffering is the discomfort brought about by resisting the pressures of the flesh. They are not physical sufferings. The law of the Spirit of life in Christ has made us free from the law of sin and death (Romans 8:2). Sickness and disease are the result of sin.

Now Begin Enjoying It

You can receive healing by the power of God, the same way you received eternal life at the new birth. It is the same power source— The Word of God.

CD 2 Outlined

I. Man is a triune being
   A. He is a spirit, he has a soul, he lives in a body
   B. The spirit receives the nature of God at the
      new birth
   C. The soul (mind, will and emotions) must be renewed to
      The Word to come in line with the spirit
   D. When the soul is in line with the spirit, the body
      will follow

II. Psalm 103:1-5—the benefits of the Lord
   A. He forgives all your sins; He heals all your diseases
   B. He redeems your life from destruction; He crowns you
      with tender love and mercy
   C. He satisfies you with good things and renews
      your youth

III. Isaiah 53:4-5
   A. Substitutionary sacrifice of the Lord Jesus Christ
   B. It was our iniquities that He was bruised for
   C. It was our sicknesses and diseases that He carried
   D. Redemption includes the forgiveness of sin and the
      healing of your body

Study Questions

(1) Why did the Psalmist David speak to his soul in Psalm 103:1? ____

_____

_____

_____

_____

(2) Explain prosperity of the soul. _____

_____

_____

_____

_____

(3) Is it the will of God for your body to be healed? _____

_____

_____

_____

_____

(4) What does it mean to be a partaker of Christ's sufferings? _____

_____

_____

_____

(5) Give two scriptural reasons why Christians may be sick. _____

_____

_____

_____

_____

Study Notes

"And the very God of peace sanctify you wholly; and I pray
God your whole spirit and soul and body be preserved blameless
unto the coming of our Lord Jesus Christ."
1 Thessalonians 5:23

3

"For the preaching of the cross is to them that perish foolishness; but unto us which are saved it is the power of God."

1 Corinthians 1:18

The Word of God must be the basis for every Christian endeavor. Therefore, The Word must be the foundation for the study of healing.

CD THREE
Study of Divine Healing I: For the World

It Is Vital to Understand the Importance of God's Word as the Foundation for Healing

The Church's Commission

FOCUS: There are three major areas in the study of divine healing. First, there is healing for the world in the Name of Jesus. Secondly, there is healing for the carnally minded Christian through prayers of the elders of the Church. And finally, there is healing for the Christian who actively enforces the fullness of his privileges in redemption.

This message deals with the first area. It instructs believers how they can take the healing power of God into the world.

The basis for every Christian endeavor should be the Word of God. Therefore, in the study of healing, The Word must be the foundation. God's Word is the incorruptible seed that is planted in the heart of a man when he hears it. The message of the Cross, or the gospel, which is God's Word, is the power of God. The Word has the power within itself to cause it to come to pass. When a person hears The Word concerning salvation, the light of that Word enters his heart and he is reborn. He cannot be reborn without having heard The Word. It is vital to understand the importance of God's Word as the foundation for healing. For it is in knowing what God has to say about it that healing can be manifest.

Healing is not just a New Testament privilege. God called Moses to write down the Old Covenant as it had been established with Abraham so the people could see it. The Israelites had lost sight of what their covenant with God was by living for so long under the bondage of Egypt. This writing consists of the first five books of the Bible. According to Deuteronomy 28, healing was promised in the old covenant.

> *Healing was manifested through Jesus because He used The Word of God, faith in God, the power of His words and the help of the Holy Spirit.*

This proves that Jesus did not introduce healing during His earthly ministry. He merely operated in the Abrahamic covenant. Philippians 2:7, literally translated, says that He emptied Himself of His divine privileges. Jesus did not use any power that is not available to every child of God today. Healing was manifested through Jesus because He used The Word of God, faith in God, the power of His words and the help of the Holy Spirit. Jesus said that the Father dwelling in Him did the works.

After Jesus ratified the New Covenant, He instructed the Church to lay hands on the sick in His Name (Mark 16:15-20). The Bible says that He will work with the believer, dwelling in him, and that He will confirm His Word by healing the sick.

Now Begin Enjoying It

The magnitude of Christianity is that God manifests Himself to the world through the believer. Every believer has the right, because of the New Testament, to lay hands on the sick in the Name of Jesus. As a co-laborer with God, he has the ability to do so through The Word of God, faith in God and the power of the Holy Spirit. The healing power of God, carried by one of God's children to the sick, is God's masterstroke of evidence that He is alive and His healing power is available today.

ℰ𝒟 3 𝒪utlined

Foundation Scripture: Mark 16:15-20

I. Three major areas of divine healing
   A. Healing for the world in Jesus' Name
   B. Healing for the carnally minded Christian
   C. Healing for the Christian who actively enforces the fullness of redemption
II. The foundation of every Christian endeavor is The Word of God
   A. The Word is incorruptible seed (1 Peter 1:23)
      1. The seed is planted in a man's heart as he hears it (2 Corinthians 4:6)
      2. The Word is the power of God (1 Corinthians 1:18)
III. Healing
   A. Was an old covenant promise (Deuteronomy 28:1-61)
   B. Jesus operated in the old covenant
      1. He emptied Himself of His divinity (Philippians 2:7)
      2. He healed through the Word of God, faith in God and the power of the Holy Spirit
IV. Healing for the world was commissioned to the Church
   A. God desires to manifest Himself through the believer
   B. Lay hands on the sick
   C. Jesus works with the believer and confirms The Word with signs following
   D. Believers today are equipped with the same power Jesus had (John 14:12)
      1. The Word, faith in God, the Holy Spirit
   E. The healing of the sick is God's masterstroke of evidence that He is alive and His healing power is available today

Study Questions

(1) Into what three major areas is divine healing divided? _____

_____

_____

_____

(2) What is the foundation for every Christian endeavor? _____

_____

_____

_____

(3) Was healing offered only during Jesus' earthly ministry? _____

_____

_____

_____

_____

(4) When Jesus healed the sick, was He functioning through His divine privileges or through the Abrahamic covenant? _____

_____

_____

_____

(5) How can the believer today have the ability to cast out devils and heal the sick? _____

_____

_____

_____

Study Notes

"*Verily, verily, I say unto you, He that believeth on me,
the works that I do shall he do also; and greater works than
these shall he do; because I go unto my Father.*"
John 14:12

4

"Is any sick among you? let him call for the elders of the church; and let them pray over him, anointing him with oil in the name of the Lord: And the prayer of faith shall save the sick, and the Lord shall raise him up; and if he have committed sins, they shall be forgiven him."

James 5:14-15

Because some Christians are ruled by their senses, God designed a way for them to receive healing.

CD FOUR

Study of Divine Healing II: Through Elders

When Jesus Went to Calvary and Paid the Price for Sin, He Paid the Price for Sickness

The Christian's Responsibility

FOCUS: How can a carnally minded Christian receive his healing? This is the second major area concerning divine healing. It is necessary to define what a carnally minded Christian is.

To be carnally minded simply means to be fleshly minded, or to be sense-ruled. A person who is controlled by his flesh is one whose mind is not renewed to the Word of God. *The Amplified Bible, Classic Edition* says he is walking as a mere man. Paul said in 1 Corinthians 3:1 that he could not talk to the church at Corinth on a spiritual level because their minds were still ruled by their five physical senses.

The sense-ruled Christian believes only what he can hear, see, feel, touch or smell. It is difficult for him to believe The Word alone because he is so accustomed to believing the knowledge that comes to him through his senses. When the physical symptoms are opposite to what The Word says, he will lean toward what sense knowledge is telling him. The Word says, "by His [Jesus'] stripes ye were healed" but his body still has pain he can *feel,* so he believes he is not healed.

When someone leans toward sense knowledge rather than what The Word says, he is unskillful in the Word. Paul told the Hebrews that they ought to be teaching others, but because they were unskillful in the Word, they still needed to be given milk rather than strong meat. They were still dependent on others to have The Word and healing ministered to them.

In receiving healing, it is vital to understand that God has done everything He's going to do. When Jesus went to Calvary and paid the price for sin, He paid the price for sickness. When Adam sinned, the curse came on the earth. The curse included sickness and disease. Galatians 3:13 says that

> *It is every Christian's responsibility to become mature and believe God's Word for himself.*

Jesus became a curse to redeem us from it. *Receiving* healing is an act of an individual's will just like *receiving* salvation. Man has been given a free will to make his own choices. When he hears The Word concerning salvation or healing, he can either receive it or reject it.

Satan has no power to keep sickness on your body once you have decided to receive the healing that has already been provided. There has to come a point when a person believes he has received it.

Now Begin Enjoying It

God desired to design a way whereby the sense-ruled Christian could *receive* his healing. The Word says in James 5:14-15 that if there is any sick among you, to call on the elders of the Church to anoint them with oil and that the prayer of faith would save the sick. This gives the person something his senses can relate to if he is not mature enough to receive healing on the basis of The Word alone. He can *feel* the oil on his head, he can *hear* the prayer of faith, he can *feel* the hands of the elders, he can *sense* the presence of others who are strong in faith. This has a tendency to strengthen his own faith, and he can believe that he has received.

This method of receiving will work for a time. However, because it has to do with the senses, there will come a time when he must stand his ground on The Word, himself. It will work. It is every Christian's responsibility to become mature and believe God's Word for himself.

$\mathcal{CD}$ 4 $\mathcal{O}utlined$

Foundation Scripture: James 5:14-15

I. Definition of carnally minded Christian
   A. Carnal—fleshly minded
      1. Ruled by knowledge received through five senses
   B. Sense-ruled person has difficulty believing The Word
      1. Is unskillful in applying The Word for himself
        (Hebrews 5:12-14)

II. Healing is available to the carnally minded Christian
   A. Through the elders of the Church (James 5:14-15)
      1. Anointing with oil
      2. Prayer of faith

III. Healing for every person is already available
   A. Each person must *receive*
      1. We are not waiting for God to heal us
      2. Jesus has redeemed us from the curse of sickness
        (Galatians 3:13; Deuteronomy 28)
   B. Receiving is an act of the will

IV. Carnal Christian tends to believe sense knowledge
   A. This is why James 5:14-15 works
      1. Gets him to the point of *believing he has received*
      2. He has something his senses relate to
        a. *feeling* of oil
        b. *hearing* the prayer of faith, etc.

V. Spiritually minded Christian is skillful in The Word
   A. Does not depend on others' faith
   B. Is not sense-ruled, but is Word-ruled
   C. This should be the goal of every Christian

$Study$ $Questions$

(1) What does it mean to be carnally minded? _____

_____

_____

_____

(2) What does a carnally minded Christian tend to believe? _____

_____

_____

_____

*(3) Explain how this kind of Christian can come to the place of **receiving** what has already been provided.* _____

_____

_____

_____

_____

(4) Why will this method not work eventually? _____

_____

_____

_____

_____

(5) What should be the goal of every Christian where healing is concerned? _____

_____

_____

_____

_____

Study Notes

"And I, bretheren, could not speak unto you as unto spiritual, but as unto carnal, even as unto babes in Christ."
1 Corinthians 3:1

5

"As newborn babes, desire the sincere milk of the word, that ye may grow thereby."

1 Peter 2:2

In the Church, the purpose of The Word of God is to allow every believer to launch out into spiritual adulthood.

CD FIVE

Study of Divine Healing III: To the Mature Christian

When sickness or disease tries to attach itself to the spiritually minded Christian, he operates the spiritual power (his faith) that is on the inside of him because *he knows* that he has already been made free from Satan's dominion.

The Spiritually Minded Man

FOCUS: The third major area in divine healing is healing for the spiritual adult. This is a Christian who walks in the fullness of his privileges in Christ.

Every born-again believer has the ability to launch out into spiritual adulthood. This is the purpose for God's Word in the Church. The Word of God is spiritual food. It produces spiritual growth just like natural food nourishes the physical body. First Peter 2:2 says, "As newborn babes, desire the sincere milk of The word, that ye may *grow thereby.*" Since the realm of the spirit is timeless, spiritual growth will come at the same rate that the spirit is fed The Word. It can grow as fast as a person desires for it to, and as much as he is willing to spend time in The Word.

When the spirit man is not fed with The Word of God, spiritual activity ceases. The spirit is eternal, so it cannot cease to exist. But, just like a muscle which is not exercised becomes dormant, the spirit will become weak. Likewise, when the spirit is properly nourished, there is no limit to how much it can grow. To the reborn man this opens up the realm of the spirit without boundary. He can grow to maturity at whatever rate he desires.

The very basis of Christianity is that God can now deal with man in the spirit. The spirit of man is that part of his triune being that has the ability to know God and fellowship with Him. Through spiritual high treason, Adam gave his authority to Satan and separated his own spirit from union with God. As a result, Satan became man's illegitimate stepfather (see John 8:44). Through Christ's death on the cross, God has provided for man's spirit to be united with Him again. As a man finds out what has happened in his spirit through

> *Every born-again believer has the ability to launch out into spiritual adulthood.*

the new birth—what he's been redeemed from and what privileges he has now because of that redemption—he can begin to allow the eternal life that is in his spirit to manifest in his mind and body. He becomes spiritually minded and changes his thinking from what he perceives through the five physical senses to what the New Testament says about him (Romans 12:2).

Living in the fullness of Christianity comes through being spiritually minded.

This is thinking in terms of spiritual law. Everything that exists is controlled by spiritual law. Romans 8:2 says, "For the law of the Spirit of life in Christ Jesus hath made me free from the law of sin and death." The law of sin and death was the result of Adam's high treason (Romans 5:17). When sickness or disease tries to attach itself to the spiritually minded Christian, he operates the spiritual power (his faith) that is on the inside of him because *he knows* that he has already been made free from Satan's dominion. He will go to The Word of God which states that he has been redeemed from the curse (Galatians 3:13) and that he has been translated out of the realm of darkness (Colossians 1:13). He will speak The Word and combat the sickness with his spiritual weapons of warfare (2 Corinthians 10:3-5). He makes The Word his final authority.

Now Begin Enjoying It

The mature Christian knows that he does not exist by bread alone but by every word which proceeds from the mouth of God (Matthew 4:4). As he chooses to believe The Word and acts on it, it will bring the results of healing to his body.

CD 5 Outlined

I. Spiritual adulthood
  A. Available to every born-again Christian (1 Peter 2:2)
  B. Comes through feeding the spirit with The Word of God
  C. Spirit realm timeless, unlimited
    1. Spiritual growth is unlimited
II. Spiritual starvation
  A. Caused by no meditation of The Word of God
  B. Causes spiritual weakness
    1. No bottom to the weakness
III. What is spiritual maturity?
  A. Spiritually minded rather than sense-ruled (Romans 12:2)
  B. Awareness of spirit realm
  C. Knowledge of redemption
    1. And rights because of redemption
  D. Spirit man in ascendancy over mind *and* body (Hebrews 5:13-14)
IV. Experiencing the *fullness* of Christianity
  A. Only by spiritually minded Christians
  B. Spiritual laws applied by:
    1. Meditation of The Word
    2. Confession of The Word
  C. Word of God final authority in believer's life
  D. Acting on The Word achieves results (James 1:25)

Study Questions

(1) What causes a Christian to grow and mature in spiritual matters?

_____

_____

(2) Why is there no limit to how fast or how much a Christian can mature spiritually? _____

_____

_____

_____

(3) Explain Romans 12:2. _____

_____

_____

_____

_____

*(4) What happens when a Christian becomes spiritually minded?*_____

_____

_____

_____

_____

(5) What law does the believer put into effect to receive the manifestation of healing in his body? _____

_____

_____

_____

Study Notes

"And be not conformed to this world: but be ye transformed
by the renewing of your mind, that ye may prove what is
that good, and acceptable, and perfect, will of God."
Romans 12:2

6

"Therefore if any man
be in Christ, he is a new
creature: old things are
passed away; behold, all
things are become new."

2 Corinthians 5:17

God's plan for Christians is for them to step
out of the realm of the natural desires
and into the realm of the spirit.

CD SIX

Study of Divine Healing IV: To the Mature Christian

The Believer Must Begin
Confessing The Word Even
When His Flesh Is Telling Him
Exactly the Opposite of What
The Word Says

Partaking of the Divine Nature

FOCUS: God's divine nature has been imparted to every born-again Christian in his inner man. "According as his divine power hath given unto us *all* things that pertain unto life and godliness, through the *knowledge* of him that hath called us to glory and virtue: Whereby are given unto us exceeding great and precious promises: *that by these* ye might be partakers of the divine nature, having escaped the corruption that is in the world through lust" (2 Peter 1:3-4).

God's plan for man is to share His life or His nature with him. By partaking of that divine nature, man can escape the corruption that is in the world. This corruption is an alteration from God's original plan. God created all things to be good. He created man in His own image. The Fall caused the perversion of everything God had made. Eve was deceived by Satan. However Adam was not—when he took sides with Eve, he committed high treason against God. Corruption came into the world.

The ultimate of Christianity is for a man to step out of the realm of his natural desires and into the realm of the spirit. This simply means to change your thinking and believing from what you perceive through your five physical senses to what The Word says. When you were born again, God imparted His life and nature into your spirit, legally. By renewing your mind with The Word—by putting off the old man, by being a doer of The Word—you can experience God's life and nature vitally. This is walking in the spirit.

The ultimate in healing for the Christian is to receive it on the basis of the exceeding great and precious promises, thereby partaking of the divine nature of God that abides in his spirit man. God calls those things which are not as though they were

> *Confessing The Word bombards Satan's barriers and knocks them down.*

(Romans 4:17). The believer must begin confessing The Word even when his flesh is telling him exactly the opposite of what The Word says. Abraham was said to have not been weak in faith when *he considered not his own body.* "He staggered not at the promise of God through unbelief but was strong in faith...being fully persuaded that, what he [God] had promised, he was able also to perform" (Romans 4:20-21).

God's Word is the sword of the spirit. Confessing and acting on The Word will cause it to come to pass.

Now Begin Enjoying It

Walking in the fullness of the privileges of Christianity is available to any who will put The Word first place in their lives. The believer who takes the exceeding great and precious promises and enforces them in his life by his actions and the words of his mouth will walk in that fullness.

𝒞𝒟 6 𝒪𝓊𝓉𝓁𝒾𝓃𝑒𝒹

I. Every born-again Christian possesses God's divine nature in his spirit man (2 Corinthians 5:17)
   A. God's purpose is for man to experience that life vitally (2 Peter 1:3)

II. Corruption that is in the world (2 Peter 1:4)
   A. Alteration of God's original plan

III. Ultimate of Christianity
   A. Escape the corruption
   B. By the promises
   C. Step out of the natural into the spiritual (Galatians 5:16)
      1. Mind renewal (Romans 12:2)
      2. Doing The Word

IV. Ultimate of healing for the Christian
   A. Receive on the basis of The Word of God
      1. Standing firm—immovable
      2. Confession of The Word
   B. Considering not the flesh (Romans 4:17)
   C. Wisdom from above (James 3:16-17)

V. Walking in the fullness of Christianity
   A. Available to every Christian

Study Questions

(1) When is the nature of God imparted to a person's inner being?_____

_____

_____

_____

(2) What is corruption?_____

_____

_____

_____

_____

(3) What was the cause of corruption coming into the world?_____

_____

_____

_____

_____

(4) How can a born-again Christian escape the corruption that is in the world? _____

_____

_____

_____

(5) Explain what it means to walk in the spirit. _____

_____

_____

_____

_____

Study Notes

"According as his divine power hath given unto us all things
that pertain unto life and godliness, through the knowledge of
him that hath called us to glory and virtue."
2 Peter 1:3

7

"And ye are complete in him, which is the head of all principality and power."

Colossians 2:10

Through your union with Christ, you can live in the freedom and dominion God planned for man.

CD SEVEN

Study of Divine Healing V: Will You Be Made Whole?

God Wants You Whole—Spirit, Soul, Body, Financially and Socially

Your Union With Christ

FOCUS: When He had completed His creation, the Bible says, "And God saw every thing that he had made, and behold, it was *very good"* (Genesis 1:31).

From the beginning, God has desired freedom for His people from the curse. It came upon the earth when Adam committed high treason.

Neither Adam's sin nor the result of it was God's will. Adam had a free will. God had made him His under-ruler in the earth. By his own will Adam made Satan his stepfather. As a result, sin, sickness, disease, poverty and want came into the earth.

The substitutionary sacrifice of the Lord Jesus Christ has delivered man from the power of darkness. Romans 8:2 says that the law of the Spirit of *life* in Christ Jesus has made us *free* from the law of *sin* and *death.* Through our union with Christ, we can live in the freedom and dominion that God originally purposed for man.

God wants you whole—spirit, soul, body, financially and socially. "And ye are complete in him [in Christ], which is the head of all principality and power" (Colossians 2:10).

You are whole through your union with Christ. Satan is the thief who comes to steal, kill and destroy (John 10:10). You have the same freedom of choice that Adam had. God's power is abundantly available to you to reign in life through Jesus Christ (Romans 5:17).

Being made whole in any area of your life demands a decision on your part.

> *The decision to be healed by the power of God must be based on our knowledge of God's willingness to use His power in our behalf.*

In John 5 is the story of the man who had been ill for 38 years. The sick would lay on their beds on five porches surrounding a pool called Bethesda. An angel would stir the water at intervals and the first sick person to step in after the troubling of the water was made whole of his disease.

Jesus saw the man lying there and asked him, "Wilt thou be made whole?" The man told Jesus that he did not have anyone to help him into the pool. But Jesus *spoke* to him and said, "Rise, take up thy bed, and walk" (John 5:8).

When Jesus spoke The Word, the power of God was available to make the man whole. He had to *decide* to be made whole. He *acted* on what Jesus said. The ninth verse says that he was *immediately* made whole.

Everything that a man receives from God, he must receive by faith. We cannot earn anything from Him. It has already been given to us through the substitutionary sacrifice of Jesus.

Now Begin Enjoying It

The *decision* to be healed by the power of God must be based on our knowledge of God's willingness to use His power in our behalf. When a man realizes, after Satan has stolen from him, that God is asking him, *"Will* you be made whole?" he can confidently say, "Yes, I *will* to be made whole."

CD 7 Outlined

I. God wants you whole
  A. God made everything good
  B. His will for us is good
  C. Satan perverted goodness through the Fall of Man

II. Healing has been provided
  A. Jesus has delivered us from the power of Satan through the cross

III. Receiving demands a decision
  A. Getting saved takes a decision
    1. "I *will* accept the price Jesus paid for me."
  B. Getting healed takes a decision
    1. "I *will* be made whole."

Study Questions

(1) *What is God's will for your life where sickness and disease are concerned?* _____

_____

_____

(2) *What is the origin of sickness and disease?* _____

_____

_____

_____

(3) *Explain the need for a decision on your part to receive from God.* _

_____

_____

_____

_____

(4) *Why will **trying** to receive healing by faith fail?* _____

_____

_____

_____

_____

(5) *On what basis can you make the decision to be made whole?* _____

_____

_____

_____

_____

Study Notes

8

"And lest I should be exalted above measure through the abundance of the revelations, there was given to me a thorn in the flesh, the messenger of Satan to buffet me, lest I should be exalted above measure."

2 Corinthians 12:7

Contrary to what religious tradition has taught,
Paul's thorn in the flesh was not a sickness.

CD EIGHT
Paul's Thorn in the Flesh

The Healing Power of God Is Available to *Anyone* Who Will Receive The Word of God and Believe It

Driving Out Religious Tradition

FOCUS: The healing power of God is available to anyone who will receive The Word of God and believe it.

Jesus is the express image of the Father God. Jesus came to the earth to do the will of God (John 5:30). God anointed Jesus with power to heal the sick (Luke 5:17). The power to heal was in His words—when He spoke to the sick, they were healed.

The New Testament is a revelation of the will of God. It is God speaking to you. You can receive The Word with as much confidence as if Jesus verbally spoke to you. God's power to heal is in His Word.

The thorn in the flesh mentioned in Paul's second letter to the Corinthians has been a hindrance to many Christians in receiving healing from God. The thorn in the flesh was not a sickness, as religious traditions have taught. This CD gives an excellent explanation of Paul's thorn from the truth of God's Word. The *truth* brings freedom.

First of all, the thorn in the flesh was *not* from God. The Apostle Paul called it *a messenger sent from Satan* to buffet him, lest he be exalted above measure through the abundance of revelations. Paul had received personal revelation of what happened in the spirit from the cross to the ascension of Jesus after His resurrection. This revelation resulted in Paul writing two-thirds of the New Testament. He has revealed to us in his epistles our inheritance *in Christ.*

> *It is God's will that you be well and whole, spirit, soul and body.*

Jesus said in Mark 4 that after The Word has been sown in a man's heart, Satan comes immediately to steal it. The thorn in the flesh was a figure of speech that Paul used to describe the evil spirit that incited persecution to hinder Paul's preaching of The Word.

In 2 Corinthians 11, Paul lists the persecutions he suffered. He was beaten, stoned and shipwrecked. He endured several types of perils and imprisonments, and experienced hunger and thirst.

Paul sought God three times, asking that the messenger of Satan depart from him. The Lord answered, "My grace is sufficient for thee: for my strength is made perfect in weakness" (2 Corinthians 12:9). The word *strength* literally means "self-energizing, explosive power." God did not refuse to deliver him. He actually said that His grace was sufficient against any danger and enabled him to bear trouble with courage. The inner resource of God's power was enough to deliver him from *anything* Satan could use to harass him. Paul later said that he therefore took pleasure in infirmities (literally: weakness, want of strength), in reproaches, in necessities, in persecutions, in distresses for Christ's or The Word's sake. When he was weak in human strength, Paul knew he was truly strong and able in divine strength.

In 2 Timothy 3:10-11, Paul said, "But thou hast fully known my doctrine, manner of life, purpose, faith, longsuffering, charity, patience, persecutions, afflictions, which came unto me at Antioch, at Iconium, at Lystra; what persecutions I endured: but *out of them all* the Lord delivered me."

Satan's messenger, the thorn in the flesh, never overcame Paul and the power of God. The messenger could do no more than harass Paul. The apostle was delivered from everything Satan tried. He was a covenant man. He knew God as his deliverer.

Now Begin Enjoying It

Allow the truth from God's Word to drive out any religious tradition that you may have in your mind concerning Paul's thorn in the flesh. You have been redeemed from the curse of sickness and disease. It is God's will that you be well and whole—spirit, soul and body.

$\mathcal{CD}$ 8 $\mathcal{O}utlined$

I. It is always the will of God to heal
  A. Jesus is the express image of God (Colossians 1:15)
  B. He was anointed of God to heal (Luke 5:17)
  C. The healing power of God is in His Word

II. Healing is available to *all;* God is no respecter
  of persons

III. Fleeces
  A. Old Testament *only*
  B. New Testament believers have the unchangeable Word
    and the Holy Spirit within to reveal it
  C. We need no confirmation other than The Word
    of God

IV. The Apostle Paul's thorn in the flesh (2 Corinthians
  12:7-9)
  A. Was not from God
  B. Was not sickness
  C. It was an evil spirit assigned to Paul by Satan to harass
    him and hinder the preaching of The Word
  D. The thorn was persecutions, perils, afflictions and worry
    1. Listed in 2 Corinthians 11:24-28
  E. God's grace was enough
    1. The power of God within Paul was enough to
      put him over in any situation
    2. Satan could not defeat him
  F. God delivered him out of them *all* (2 Timothy 3:10-11)

Study Questions

(1) Explain why the New Testament believer does not need a fleece to confirm God's Word to receive his healing. _____

_____

_____

(2) Was Paul's thorn in the flesh a sickness? _____

_____

_____

_____

(3) Why does Satan come immediately to steal The Word from the believer's heart? _____

_____

_____

_____

_____

*(4) What actually **was** the thorn in the flesh?* _____

_____

_____

_____

(5) Did God deliver the Apostle Paul from his persecutions? _____

_____

_____

_____

_____

Study Notes

"And he said unto me, My grace is sufficient for thee: for my strength
is made perfect in weakness. Most gladly therefore will I rather glory
in my infirmities, that the power of Christ may rest upon me."
2 Corinthians 12:9

Prayer for Salvation and Baptism in the Holy Spirit

Heavenly Father, I come to You in the Name of Jesus. Your Word says, "Whosoever shall call on the name of the Lord shall be saved" (Acts 2:21). I am calling on You. I pray and ask Jesus to come into my heart and be Lord over my life according to Romans 10:9-10: "If thou shalt confess with thy mouth the Lord Jesus, and shalt believe in thine heart that God hath raised him from the dead, thou shalt be saved. For with the heart man believeth unto righteousness; and with the mouth confession is made unto salvation." I do that now. I confess that Jesus is Lord, and I believe in my heart that God raised Him from the dead. I repent of sin. I renounce it. I renounce the devil and everything he stands for. Jesus is my Lord.

I am now reborn! I am a Christian—a child of Almighty God! I am saved! You also said in Your Word, "If ye then, being evil, know how to give good gifts unto your children; HOW MUCH MORE shall your heavenly Father give the Holy Spirit to them that ask him?" (Luke 11:13). I'm also asking You to fill me with the Holy Spirit. Holy Spirit, rise up within me as I praise God. I fully expect to speak with other tongues as You give me the utterance (Acts 2:4). In Jesus' Name. Amen!

Begin to praise God for filling you with the Holy Spirit. Speak those words and syllables you receive—not in your own language, but the language given to you by the Holy Spirit. You have to use your own voice. God will not force you to speak. Don't be concerned with how it sounds. It is a heavenly language!

Continue with the blessing God has given you and pray in the spirit every day.

You are a born-again, Spirit-filled believer. You'll never be the same!

Find a good church that boldly preaches God's Word and obeys it. Become part of a church family who will love and care for you as you love and care for them.

We need to be connected to each other. It increases our strength in God. It's God's plan for us.

Make it a habit to watch the Believer's Voice of Victory Network and become a doer of the Word, who is blessed in his doing (James 1:22-25).

About the Author

Kenneth Copeland is co-founder and president of Kenneth Copeland Ministries in Fort Worth, Texas, and best-selling author of books that include *Honor—Walking in Honesty, Truth and Integrity*, and *THE BLESSING of The LORD Makes Rich and He Adds No Sorrow With It*.

Since 1967, Kenneth has been a minister of the gospel of Christ and teacher of God's Word. He is also the artist on award-winning albums such as his Grammy-nominated *Only the Redeemed, In His Presence, He Is Jehovah, Just a Closer Walk* and *Big Band Gospel*. He also co-stars as the character Wichita Slim in the children's adventure videos *The Gunslinger, Covenant Rider* and the movie *The Treasure of Eagle Mountain*, and as Daniel Lyon in the Commander Kellie and the Superkids™ videos *Armor of Light* and *Judgment: The Trial of Commander Kellie*. Kenneth also co-stars as a Hispanic godfather in the 2009 and 2016 movies *The Rally* and *The Rally 2: Breaking the Curse*.

With the help of offices and staff in the United States, Canada, England, Australia, South Africa and Ukraine, Kenneth is fulfilling his vision to boldly preach the uncompromised WORD of God from the top of this world, to the bottom, and all the way around. His ministry reaches millions of people worldwide through daily and Sunday TV broadcasts, magazines, teaching audios and videos, conventions and campaigns, and the World Wide Web.

Learn more about Kenneth Copeland Ministries
by visiting our website at **kcm.org**

When The LORD first spoke to Kenneth and Gloria Copeland about starting the *Believer's Voice of Victory* magazine...

He said: *This is your seed. Give it to everyone who ever responds to your ministry, and don't ever allow anyone to pay for a subscription!*

For more than 50 years, it has been the joy of Kenneth Copeland Ministries to bring the good news to believers. Readers enjoy teaching from ministers who write from lives of living contact with God, and testimonies from believers experiencing victory through God's WORD in their everyday lives.

Today, the *BVOV* magazine is mailed monthly, bringing encouragement and blessing to believers around the world. Many even use it as a ministry tool, passing it on to others who desire to know Jesus and grow in their faith!

Request your FREE subscription to the *Believer's Voice of Victory* magazine today!

Go to **freevictory.com** to subscribe online, or call us at **1-800-600-7395** (U.S. only) or **+1-817-852-6000**.